# Home Building For the Wise Woman

## A Blueprint for Designing a Life That Fits

Linda D. Schwartz

*Live New! Press*
*Berne, Indiana*

> *Dedicated to Anita Wenger,*
> *my Titus 2 friend.*

Copyright © 2015 by Linda D. Schwartz. All rights reserved. No part of this book may be reproduced or transmitted in any form or by any means, electronic or mechanical, including photocopying, recording, or by any information storage and retrieval system, without written permission from the publisher, with the exception of the blank diagrams for personal use. Published by Live New! Press, 866 Clark St., Berne, IN 46711.

Printed by CreateSpace, An Amazon.com Company

Cover Design: Nicole E. Dynes
Illustrated by: Nicole E. Dynes

Special thanks to Nicole Dynes for editing this study. To Don Williams and Kate Uebersax for offering your perspectives. And to Pat and Katie Harris for encouraging me to write.

Scripture quotations taken from The Holy Bible, New International Version® NIV®
Copyright © 1973, 1978, 1984, 2011 by Biblica, Inc.™
Used by permission. All rights reserved worldwide.

ISBN-13: 978-0-692-53241-6 (Live New! Press)
ISBN-10: 0692532412

# Contents

1 Survey the Site ---------------------------------------------------- 5

2 Footer and Foundation --------------------------------------- 10

3 Bearing Walls ----------------------------------------------------- 19

4 A Roof over Your Head -------------------------------------- 26

5 Interior Walls ----------------------------------------------------- 36

6 Furniture and Décor ------------------------------------------ 45

7 Build Your Lovely Home ------------------------------------ 51

# 1
# Survey the Site

*The wise woman builds her house, but with her own hands the foolish one tears hers down. Proverbs 14:1*

Think about everything that comprises a home. The people, pets, atmosphere, appearance. The furnishings, friends, finances. The meals, lawn, vehicles. That's a lot to manage—and a lot to mess up! How do we as women go about building all the areas of our home and avoid tearing them down?

I struggle to understand how the different facets of my life fit together—when to give one priority over the other. It's hard for me to grasp when it's okay for something that is less important to take center stage over something that is a top priority. But that's how life works. The cat gets sick and has to go to the vet; and hubby comes home to a messy house and no supper. My all-or-nothing mentality says I've failed, and I feel guilty and defeated. I think, "If I was a good manager, supper would be on and the house neat, no matter what." Good management might keep the mess to a minimum, but did I fail? No, I did what I had to do.

In this Bible study, you will develop a blueprint that will help you understand how a sick cat fits in with everything else in your life. It is a tool you can use to make wise decisions. My prayer is that God will work through this study to get rid of that lousy feeling of failure in the pit of your stomach and the guilt that robs you of your joy.

You may wonder, why a blueprint? The blueprint idea came about after a visit with a friend. We were discussing God's priorities for us and were exploring ways to represent the concept visually. I was familiar with the numerical list idea. You know, 1) God, 2) Husband, 3) Kids, 4) Home, 5) Others. But, I struggled with what happens when number five takes precedence over number two, for example. My friend preferred a picture with three concentric circles representing God, family, and others. Any given day was like a slice of pie including a bit of all three circles. Like I said, I am an all-or-nothing thinker, so circles had me, well, going in circles.

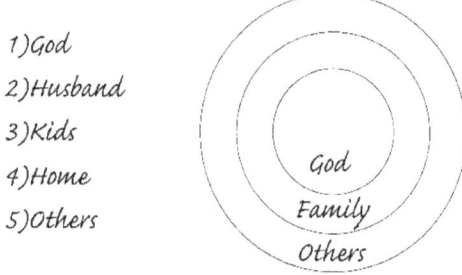

After our visit I asked God to give me a way of visualizing his priorities for me in a way I could understand. The home-building analogy was an answer to that prayer.

Early in our marriage, my husband, Doug, and I built a house together. We hired a contractor for some of the work, but we did a lot of it ourselves. From that experience, I learned that some parts of a house are essential. Others are optional. Some things must be done right away; others can be left until later. We moved in with no carpet or trim, no stove, and no railing surrounding the stairway to the basement—not the best idea, but we got along without it, temporarily.

In the same way, we must build our homes (not just our houses, but our lives) according to God's plan if we want to please him and show his glory. And, as with our house, there are opportunities and activities in our lives we can let go, either temporarily or for good. And one way of picturing how all the aspects of our lives fit together is by using a cross-section of a house. For the sake of this study, we will call it our "blueprint." It's not a plan one would use to build an actual structure, but we're building homes, not houses, right? So it's okay.

At the back of this book are blank copies of a blueprint for you to fill out. You may want to make copies for future use because, as you will see, this plan is always changing. Examples of how to fill in each area of the blueprint follow each section of this study, and there is a completed copy at the back of the book for your reference.

***

Before the building of our house began, Doug and I walked around the lot and got a feel for the "lay of the land." Where was the high ground? Were there any low spots that would create a drainage problem? What were the best locations for the well and the septic?

Similarly, in preparing to build your home, it is helpful to evaluate where you are right now. In this way you will see where you are succeeding and where you need to improve. So, take a few moments to survey your "building site" by answering these questions.

1) About whom or what am I most passionate?
_____
_____
_____

2) On what or with whom do I spend most of my time?
_____
_____
_____

3) In what areas of my life do I experience confusion, fear, guilt, chaos, or conflict?
_____
_____
_____

4) In what areas of my life do I feel capable, blessed, or at peace?
_____
_____
_____

As you reflected on these questions, did you think of some things that are out of whack? Hang on. After going through this study, you'll have a tool to help you make positive changes.

5) Look at Psalm 119:18. Who is the psalmist depending on to help him understand God's word?

_____

6) Find 1 Corinthians 2:11-12. Who knows what you are thinking?

_____

7) Who knows what God is thinking?

_____

8) So, how can we understand God's plan for our life and our home?

_____

_____

_____

As you go through this study, pray for God's Spirit to open your eyes to see how you can build a life that fits—a life that fits his plan, and that fits you and your family. Now that we've surveyed our site, let's look at step one of wise home building.

# 2
# Footer and Foundation

*Therefore everyone who hears these words of mine and puts them into practice is like a wise man who built his house on the rock. Matthew 7:24*

**Connect to the Rock**
Before Doug and I built our house—even before we laid the foundation—the contractor had to pour the footers. A footer is the connection between the foundation of a house and the rock below. A trench is dug down to solid ground and gravel is poured into it and compacted. Then the trench is filled with cement. This provides a firm base for the foundation that will be laid.

In Matthew 7, Jesus told a story about two builders. One built his house on sand, but when a storm came, the house fell with a great crash. Imagine the jumble of timbers, rafters, wallpaper, and furniture—all in a soggy heap! Without having its foundation on rock, a house is susceptible to shifting and sinking. The wise man built his house on rock, and when the storm came, the house stood "because it had its foundation on the rock."

In our lives, what is the rock we must build upon? Matthew 16:13-19 tells us that faith in Jesus, the Son of God, is the rock upon which God's Church is built. John 14:6 puts it another way: "Jesus answered, 'I am the way and the truth and the life. No one comes to the Father except through me.'" We all have done, thought or said things that go against what God wants (Romans 3:23). The Bible calls this sin, and sin separates us from God and leads to eternal death (Romans 6:23). But God provided a way for us to be reconciled to him. He sent Jesus to die on the cross as payment for our sin, so that, through faith in Jesus, we may be forgiven for all our sins. John 1:12 says, "Yet to all who did receive him, to those who believed in his name, he gave the right to become children of God . . . ." How amazing!

1) Read Romans 5:8. How does God show his love for us?

_____

_____

_____


2) In John 3:16, we see that God gave Jesus so we can have eternal life. What must we do to get this life?

_____

_____

_____


3) Ephesians 2:3 says that before believing in Christ as our Savior, "we were by nature deserving of wrath." Look at John 1:12 again. How does our relationship with God change when we receive Christ?

_____

_____

_____

_____

4) In 1 John 5:13, what can we be sure of when we believe in Jesus?

_____

_____

Through faith in Jesus, you can have a relationship with your Creator! When you trust Christ as your Savior and become his follower, he provides a firm base on which to build your life and your home. He is the "footer".

If you have not set your feet on the solid rock that is Jesus Christ but are ready to put your faith in him, I invite you to stop reading and talk to God about this right now. If you have already made this decision, take this opportunity to thank God for his amazing gift! Turn to your personal blueprint at the back of the book. In the footer, write the date of your decision to trust Christ or a note of thanks for the gift of a relationship with God.

**Lay a Solid Foundation**
Some houses have a crawl space and others are built on a cement slab. Doug and I had a basement under the home we built. Whatever foundation is used, the principle is the same. Cement is poured on top of the footers, giving the builder a solid base on which to erect the home.

Once we have dug down to the rock and poured the footer of faith, we can lay the foundation of our life. Jesus said the most important command God has given us is to love him with everything we are (Matthew 22:35-38). In Deuteronomy 5:7, God tells us, "You shall have no other gods before me." We should treasure God more than our husband, our children, our home, our job, or our friends.

When we allow something or someone to become more important than God, it harms our relationship with God and others, and it creates chaos. Jesus said in Matthew 6:33, "But seek first his kingdom and his righteousness . . . ." The exciting thing about this is that when we put God first, we won't be missing out, but will find true life. In John 17:3, Jesus said, "Now this is eternal life: that they know you, the only true God, and Jesus Christ, whom you have sent."

Loving God is a lifelong process. I am still on the journey to loving him more, but I have found a few principles to be important in moving me in that direction.

1) The Bible is vital in growing our love of God.
a. Look up Psalm 119:11. How can we avoid sinning?

_____

_____

_____

b. What are ways you can hide God's word in your heart?

_____

_____

_____

Spending time in God's word is crucial. If you're not a strong reader, find another way to get the Bible into your heart. Read a children's Bible story book, listen to sermons, or think about passages you have heard. Sing or listen to scriptural songs. The Bible is a huge part of how we learn what pleases God. Make an effort to get it into your life.

2) Submit to God in everything.
   a. Read Proverbs 3:5-6. Whom should we trust?
   _____

   _____

   b. How should we trust him?
   _____

   _____

   c. What should we not trust?
   _____

   _____

   d. In what parts of our life should we submit to God?
   _____

   _____

   _____

   e. How will God respond to our submission?
   _____

   _____

   _____

If we want God's direction, we need to be ready to do everything his way. Submitting to God in all our ways includes taking all our concerns to him. Is the baby crying nonstop? Ask God to help. Is the computer glitchy? Pray. Do you need to talk with your husband about the budget? Ask

God to prepare his heart and watch over your mouth. Is the puppy difficult to housetrain? Ask God for insight. 1 Peter 5:7 tells us, "Cast all your anxiety on him because he cares for you." God is always with his children and ready to help them.

3) We must rely on his Spirit.
a. Look up John 15:5. What does Jesus say is the result of remaining in him?

_____

_____

_____

b. What can we do on our own?

_____

_____

Jesus said in John 14:26, "But the Advocate, the Holy Spirit, whom the Father will send in my name, will teach you all things and will remind you of everything I have said to you." Throughout your day, I encourage you to keep an ear tuned to the Holy Spirit, ready to hear—and follow—His leading. What an exciting way to live!

4) We need each other.
a. Find Hebrews 10:24-25. What does it mean to "spur one another on?"

_____

_____

_____

b. What are we to urge one another to do?

_____
_____
_____

c. What is the purpose of getting together with other Christians?

_____
_____
_____

I have found the teaching and example of other Christ-followers to be essential in moving me closer to God. Do you know someone who is further along in an area in which you want to grow? Why not ask her to meet with you over coffee and share her insight?

Some time back, I chose to focus on the goal of loving God more. As a step toward that goal, I asked a woman I perceived as loving God to meet with me and share the things that had moved her in that direction. She came well prepared. As we walked the footpath around our local retirement center, we enjoyed a special time of discipleship. Much of what she taught me I have shared with you—the body of Christ at work!

We have just scratched the surface of what it means to love God with all that we are, but deciding that he is our most important pursuit is foundational to building our homes wisely. As a reminder to seek God first, turn to your blueprint and write "Love God" in the foundation. You can also copy your favorite verse from this section onto your foundation. Or jot down ideas of how you plan to improve your relationship with God.

Now that this firm foundation is drawn into our plan, let's lay out walls.

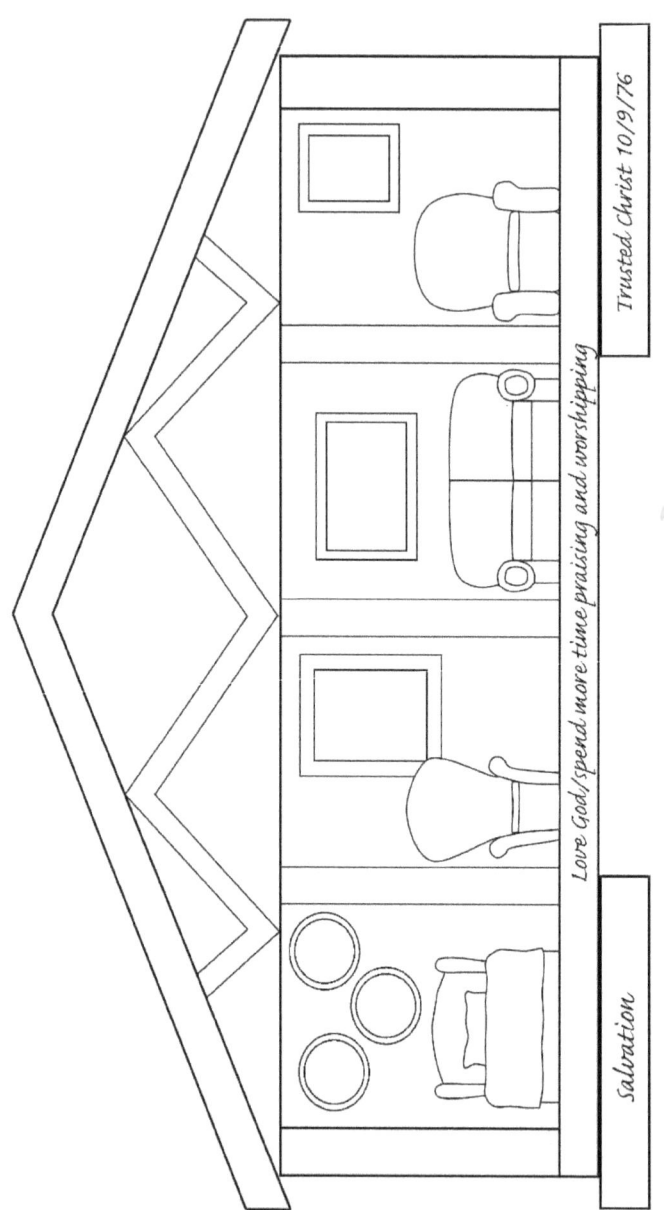

# 3
# Bearing Walls

*Jesus replied: "'Love the Lord your God with all your heart and with all your soul and with all your mind.' This is the first and greatest commandment. And the second is like it: 'Love your neighbor as yourself.' All the law and the Prophets hang on these two commandments." Matthew 22:37-40*

In a house, the most important walls are called load-bearing walls. These walls have to be strong and cannot be removed or the integrity of the house is endangered. The bearing walls need to be built before the roof can be installed and must be placed properly to conduct the weight of the roof down to the foundation.

In Matthew 22:37-40, Jesus tells us that all of God's righteous requirements are summed up in the commands to love God and love others. Look again at John 15. After Jesus says we must remain in him to bear fruit, he tells us in verses 9-11 to obey his commands. And then he funnels it down to one thing. "My command is this: Love each other as I have loved you. Greater love has no one than this: to lay down one's life for one's friends." (v12) We are rarely called upon to die physically for another, but there are other ways we should lay down our lives.

**Treat People Right**
Look up Matthew 7:12. What are ways you can do this with family members, coworkers, or friends?

_____

_____

Many people are familiar with this instruction, called "the golden rule." But when reminded of it, a common response is, "Well, yeah, but . . . ." Don't let yourself make excuses for why someone doesn't deserve to be treated the way you want to be treated. Yes, the guy at work is arrogant. But if you wouldn't want to be left out of the break room birthday party, don't exclude him. Jesus didn't say, "Do to others what you would have them do to you, as long as they are easy to get along with." Ephesians 4:2 says, "Be completely humble and gentle; be patient, bearing with one another in love." The Greek word for "bearing with" is also translated "put up with" and "endure." God knows we all can be difficult to get along with at times. Maybe, instead of the "Golden Rule," we should call it the "No Excuses Rule!"

**Serve Others**
1) In Galatians 5:13, what are we called to be?
_____

2) How are we supposed to use our freedom?
_____

_____

_____

When my children were babies, I was unsatisfied with the level of Doug's involvement in their care. I nagged him about helping with their baths and looked down on him because he wasn't into all the nurturing stuff. I focused on ways he didn't meet my needs and it caused stress in our marriage. Then I realized that I was asking Doug to be someone he was not. When I changed my focus to how I could support him and how I could meet his needs, everything changed! I saw how much Doug did for me (tons!) and felt secure in his love. And the cool thing is, Doug became more willing to help with the babies. Serving one another, instead of dwelling on our own needs, brings joy and peace to a relationship.

This does not mean we should enable others to continue in destructive or sinful behaviors. Notice that this scripture says to serve one another in love. Loving others sometimes requires confrontation and conflict. Our goal should be to move them closer to God's best for them.

**Use Healthy Words**
1) Read Ephesians 4:29. What kind of words should we speak?

___

___

2) What purpose should our words fulfill?

___

___

Unwholesome is defined as injurious or unhealthy. I have often heard this verse applied to swear words. And I understand that vulgar language does not promote moral health. But this means so much more! I can use proper English, yet destroy someone with a rumor. It's easy to tell my kids their mistakes and forget to praise their successes.

First Thessalonians 5:11 tells us to "encourage one another and build each other up." A friend of mine once mentioned that part of her role as a mom was to keep up her children's spirits. That's our job as members of God's family, too!

3) What are ways you can encourage someone with words?
___
___
___

We also can build each other up through music. Ephesians 5:19 tells us to speak "to one another with psalms, hymns, and songs from the Spirit."

4) If you can sing or play an instrument what are ways you can use that to encourage others? If the only thing you know how to play is your mp3 player, how can you use that tool to strengthen a friend?
___
___
___

**Forgive Like God Does**
1) In Ephesians 4:32, what three character traits are we to have?
___
___

2) Regarding forgiving, what pattern are we supposed to follow?
___
___

Wouldn't it be great if no one ever offended or hurt us? Unfortunately, that's not how it is in a fallen world. I think it is especially hard to cope when fellow believers hurt us. They're supposed to be following God! But we are all in process toward becoming more like Jesus. And the fact is, we haven't arrived yet. So how do we handle it when we are hurt?

Jesus told the story of a servant who owed his king twenty years' wages. He wasn't able to pay it back, and the king ordered him, his family, and all he had to be sold to repay the debt. The servant begged for time and said he would pay the debt in full (not likely). The king mercifully canceled the debt. After this, the man went to a fellow servant who owed him one day's wages. Rather than let his friend off the hook, as you would expect, he demanded to be repaid. When the fellow servant could not pay him, the man had him thrown into prison! When the king heard this, he was livid. He ordered the man to be tortured until he could pay back all he owed.

This is how God sees it when we are unwilling to forgive others. He has forgiven us a debt we could never pay. Not only that, but he gave his Son's life to do so! How dare we not forgive each other! This story tells us how serious forgiveness is to God. It shows that remembering what God has done for us helps us to forgive others. Just remember, Jesus said we can do nothing apart from him. He will help us.

In the same way that the load-bearing walls support the weight of a house and transfer that weight to the foundation, love for others supports all our relationships and activities. We can love others well only when love for

God is the foundation of everything we do. Colossians 3:14 says it this way: "And over all these virtues put on love, which binds them all together in perfect unity." Go to your blueprint and write the word LOVE on the bearing walls. If you want to focus on a particular aspect of love for God or others, write it on the walls, too.

Now that you have all the supporting structures placed on your blueprint, it's time to add a roof.

# Bearing Walls

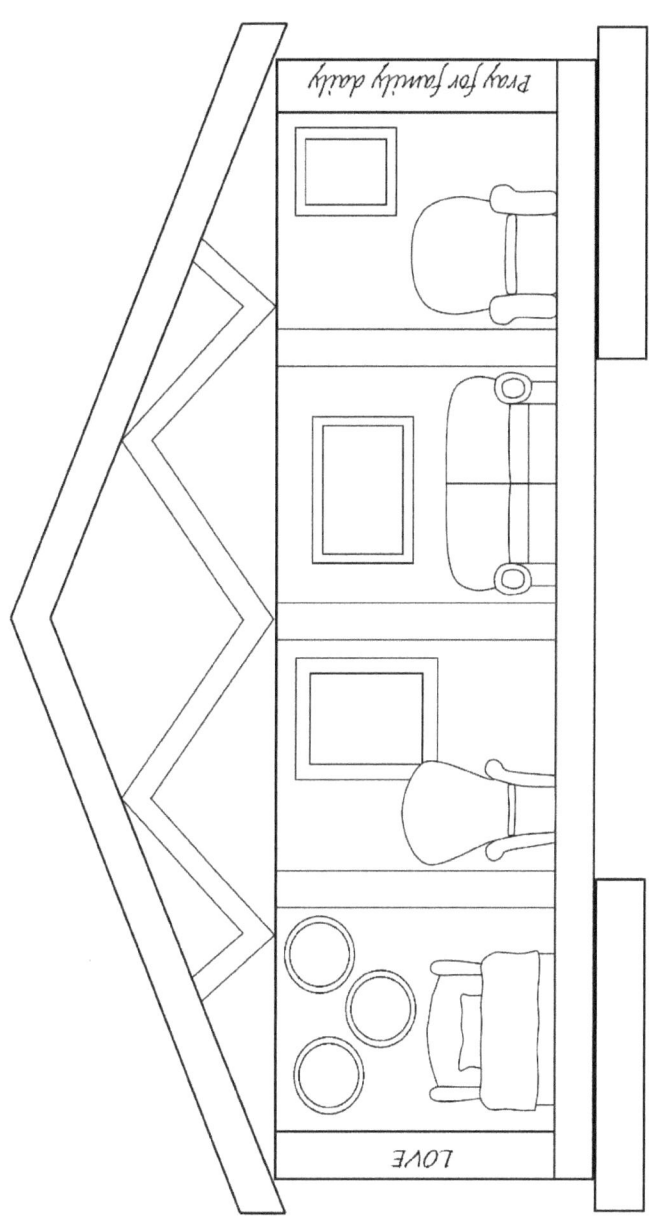

# 4
# A Roof over Your Head

*An unmarried woman or virgin is concerned about the Lord's affairs: Her aim is to be devoted to the Lord in both body and spirit. But a married woman is concerned about ... how she can please her husband. 1 Corinthians 7:34*

Even though the contractor had laid the foundation and built the bearing walls, Doug and I couldn't finish the inside of our house until we added the roof. Without the roof everything inside the house was exposed to the elements.

**Identify Your Roof**
God has provided a "roof" in our lives, an authority structure, for our security and protection. The specifics of our roof can vary, depending on whether we are married or single, on our own or still living with our parents. But for all of us, the roof represents an overarching priority in our lives—a God-given authority designed to nurture and protect us. Abuse of power, pride, and the influence of western culture make it difficult to obey the command to submit to authority. But God's design for authority is healthy and beautiful. Let's first look at God's design for authority and then we will see how that works out in our own lives.

1) Authority in Society
a. Look at Romans 13:1-7. With what authority is this passage dealing?

_____

_____

b. Who sets up government?




c. Rebelling against government is actually rebelling against whom?




d. In verse 4, what is the purpose of government?




e. What attitude is required toward authority in verse 7?




f. These concepts are reinforced in 1 Peter 2:11-17. In verses 12 and 15, what results from our obedience to authority?




2) Authority in the Church
a. Read Ephesians 5:21-33. In verse 23, who is the head of the church?

b. Verses 25-29 tell how Christ leads the church. How does Christ exercise his authority over the church?

_____

_____

_____

_____

c. What is to be the church's response in verse 24?

_____

_____

d. God has also established human leaders in the church. These leaders are responsible to keep watch over the spiritual welfare of the believers. Hebrews 13:17 tells us two attitudes we should have toward our church leaders. What are they?

_____

_____

e. What is the outcome of submitting to our leaders?

_____

_____

f. What is the result for us?

_____

_____

g. In Mark 10:42-45, Jesus explains the requirement for church leaders. What is the leader's role?

h. How did Jesus model this?

3) Authority in the Home
a. In Ephesians 6:1-4, children are told to obey their parents. What kind of leadership are parents supposed to give?

b. The pattern for leadership in marriage is portrayed in Ephesians 5:22-33. In what way is a wife supposed to submit to her husband?

c. What is the husband's role in regard to his wife?

The recurring theme in the above passages is servant leadership. Submission to authority is not an issue of God valuing one person over another. Godly leadership brings order and mutual benefit. That authority is a joy to submit to!

How can you identify the roof in your life? In Numbers 30, God instructs the Israelites about vows made by women. Though we are not under the Mosaic Law, there is a principal we can learn from this passage. If a young woman living at home made a vow, her father could overrule her promise and God would not hold it against her. A married woman's husband could also nullify her vow with no consequences. But a widowed or divorced woman's vow was binding. If we put this together with what we learned in Ephesians about authority in the home, we conclude the following. If you are married, your authority is your husband. If you are young, single and live with your parents, your authority is your father. If you're on your own, the roof over your head is God himself.

On your blueprint, write the primary authority God has placed in your life in the roof space. You may want to write other authorities in your life (pastor, elders, boss, etc.) on the trusses below the roof to remind you of resources that God has provided for your benefit.

**The Husband-Wife Relationship**
We've already studied ways to nurture our relationship with God. Now let's look more closely at the husband-wife relationship.

1) Two Examples to Follow
Find 1 Peter 3:1. The first sentence tells wives to submit to their husband "in the same way." That indicates we need to go back to an earlier passage to see how wives are to submit.

a. Look at 1 Peter 2:18-25. In verse 18, what are slaves instructed to do?

_____

_____

b. Are they supposed to submit only to masters that are considerate?

_____

_____

c. In verse 20, what is commendable before God?

_____

_____

d. Verse 21 begins another example. In whose steps should we follow?

_____

e. In verse 23, what two things did Jesus not do?

_____

_____

f. What did he do instead?

_____

_____

Peter says that wives should submit to their husbands in the same way that slaves should submit to masters and that Christ submitted to the will of the Father. Peter is not saying that women should tolerate abuse. But, what we can take away is that we should do good; and when our husband's behavior is less than stellar, we should not retaliate.

2) True Beauty
a. With this context in mind, read 1 Peter 3:1-6. In verse 1, by what are unbelieving husbands won over to faith in Christ?

_____

_____

b. Without what?

_____

c. In verse 2, what behavior should a wife display?

_____

_____

Reverence is a feeling of profound respect and love. When a man receives reverence, rather than nagging, he is free to change his mind and grow.

d. In verse 4, from where should our beauty come?

_____

_____

_____

This is not teaching that women can't wear jewelry or nice clothes. The woman of noble character in Proverbs 31 dressed in fine clothing. And there are other examples like this in the Old Testament. But this verse does teach an emphasis on inward beauty.

e. In verse 6, what two things can we do to be like Sarah, who was considered beautiful into her old age?

_____

_____

_____

Have you ever thought about what it means to "not give way to fear?" This fear does not refer to being afraid of one's husband. It involves not trusting in his judgment or, ultimately, in God's provision. We can't give in to that. We have to do what's right and trust God (and our husband) with the outcome. Notice we are right back to the example of Jesus that we looked at in chapter two of 1 Peter. He committed no sin and he entrusted himself to God.

How does this submission work out on a daily, practical level? When Doug and I installed the shingles on our new house, we were careful to cover every nail with another shingle to prevent leaks. Over the years we maintained the roof, repairing damage as soon as it occurred. Even a small leak can cause a lot of destruction inside a house.

A marriage also requires constant care and attention. Resolve conflict as quickly as possible. Practice the principles you learned in the section on love. I recommend that you periodically ask your husband what you can do for him. The answer may surprise you and it will help clarify your choices as you go through your day. I asked Doug what housecleaning task mattered most to him. He said he didn't mind if the house was dusty, but clutter bothered him. So if I have to choose between picking up and dusting, I clear the clutter. I also know that my tendency to have a quick retort bothers him. That might not bother a man that enjoys a good debate. So I can't tell you the specifics of how to respect and submit to your husband. I'll leave that wonderful adventure to you!

I encourage you to think about how you can live out this submission to your "roof," whether that be your father, God, or your husband. As you learn new ways to do that, jot your ideas on the roof of your blueprint as a reminder.

We've got a lot accomplished on our home building project! Vital structures are in place. Now let's design the interior.

# A Roof over Your Head

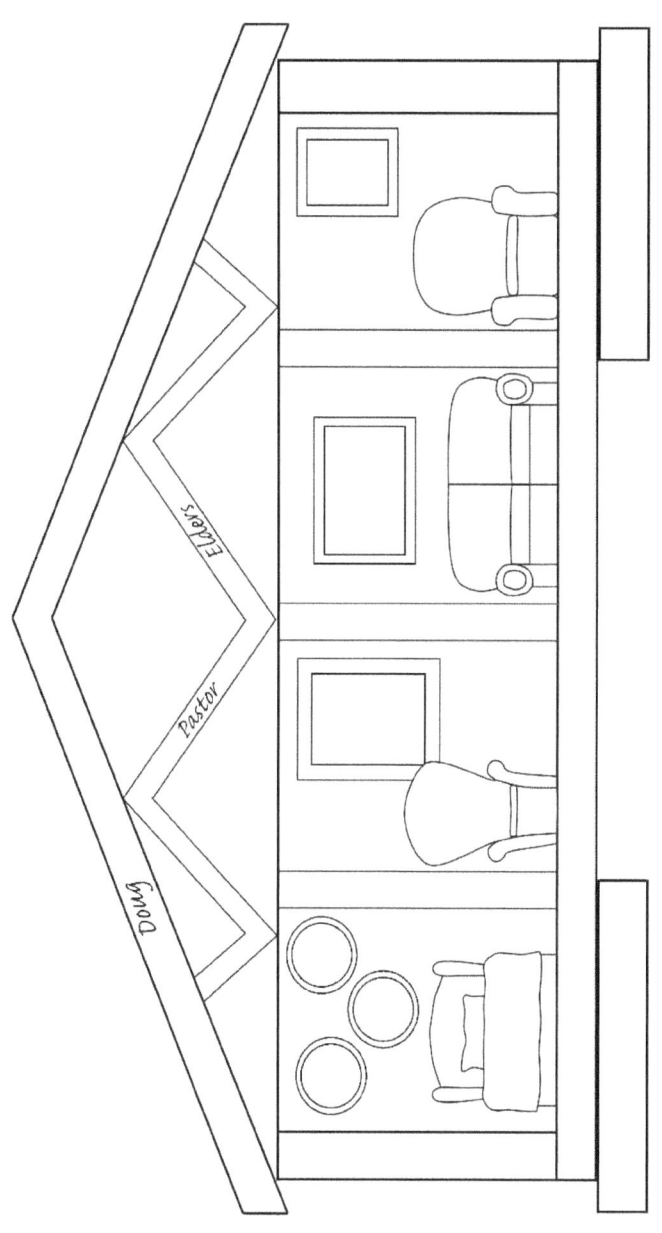

# 5
# Interior Walls

*Then [the older women] can urge the younger women to love their husbands and children, to be self-controlled and pure, to be busy at home, to be kind . . . Titus2:4-5*

In a house, non-load-bearing walls can be added or removed, designing the space to accommodate the homeowner's needs. Doug and I recently added a dividing wall in our combination breezeway-laundry room, creating a separate laundry room and a more inviting foyer. We don't take on remodeling projects often; they're difficult and messy. But in time, our aching backs heal and the new change becomes normal.

Like interior walls, our next priorities are long-term but not necessarily permanent. They give shape and structure to our lives. For example, when my children were young, they took precedence (after Doug). But, now, my children are grown and one of my main concerns is my aging father. One challenge with these callings is knowing when it's time to take out a "wall" and build a new one. When we understand what is important to God, we are better able to set wise priorities and know when it is time to remodel. Let's explore the "walls" God talks about in his word.

**Raising Children**
In Ephesians 6:4, parents are commanded to bring up their children in the training and instruction of the Lord. Let's look at three components of godly parenting.

1) Discipline
a. Read Hebrews 12:7-11. What does the writer of Hebrews assume about parents and their children?

_____

_____

_____

_____

b. In verses 10-11, what is the purpose of God's discipline?

_____

_____

_____

_____

c. The purpose of discipline is not to punish, but to influence future behavior. Look at Proverbs 29:15. What happens if parents fail to train and discipline their child?

_____

_____

_____

None of us will discipline perfectly, but we can work at being consistent, and trust God to help us see this job through.

2) Teaching
Find Deuteronomy 6:6-7. With what important task are parents entrusted?

_____

Teaching our children about God is an awesome responsibility and a great privilege. But if we isolate teaching our children from the rest of this instruction in verses 5-9, we come up short. Here again, love for God is emphasized. God wants us to keep him in the forefront of our thinking.

Colossians 3:21 says, "Fathers, do not embitter your children, or they will become discouraged." We can embitter our children by being inconsistent in discipline, by allowing our priorities to get messed up, and by expecting one standard for our kids and another for ourselves. Kids aren't fooled by a "do as I say, not as I do" approach.

3) Comfort
a. In Isaiah 66:13 what picture does God use to describe his care for Israel?

_____

_____


b. In 1 Thessalonians 2:7-8, Paul talks of how gentle he was in dealing with the Thessalonians. How did he describe this for them?

_____

_____


An important role of parents is that of comforter. By balancing comfort, discipline, and teaching, we will be well on our way toward bringing our children up "in the training and instruction of the Lord." (Ephesians 6:4)

## Managing a Home

1) In Titus 2:4-5, Paul tells Titus what older women should impress upon younger women. List the qualities that bring honor to God.

_____

_____

_____

_____

Let's consider what it means to be busy at home.

2) Proverbs 31 gives us a snapshot of a woman of noble character. In verse 27, want does this woman do?

_____

_____

3) What does she avoid?

_____

The word idle means not busy or avoiding work. In 1 Timothy 5:14, Paul instructed young widows to "marry, to have children, to manage their homes and to give the enemy no opportunity for slander." This was in contrast to some women's habit of "being idle and going about from house to house" in verse 13.

This gal in Proverbs 31 was consistent (verse 11), worked hard (verse 17), and provided food (verse 15) and clothing (verse 21) for her household. I struggle with being consistent and diligent. I'm not a person who can't sit still. Believe me, I can sit still! One passage of scripture that has helped me is Proverbs 6:9-11.

4) To whom is this warning addressed?
_____

5) What is he told to stop doing?
_____

_____

6) What will be the result if he continues being lazy?
_____

_____

_____

This passage is not condemning sleep. We need to restore our bodies through a good night's rest. It is talking about sleeping or doing nothing when we should be working. Let's suppose the sluggard is a farmer. What is the result of goofing off when he should plant, weed, or harvest? It's easy to see how poverty is the natural outcome.

But what about taking care of a house? How can failing to do the laundry, clean house, cook, or do the dishes result in poverty? The poverty that occurs is the loss of peace, health, and renewal that a well-managed home provides. And this verse says it can sneak up on you! If this is an area of struggle for you, I suggest you read a home management book like *The Messies Manual*, by Sandra Felton, or visit www.flylady.net. Both have helped me to improve in this area.

Be willing to think outside the box to bring order to your home. The woman in Proverbs 31 didn't do everything. She had servants to help her. You might share tasks with other family members. Consider hiring outside help if the budget allows. Streamline housework by getting rid of excess belongings. You could even consider downsizing to a home that is easier to manage. How you achieve an ordered home is up to you. The main thing is to make it happen.

**Caring for Parents**
Read 1 Timothy 5:4-8, 16. In verse 4, what is pleasing to God?

_____

_____

_____

From Jesus' teaching in Mark 7:9-13, we learn that the command to honor our father and mother refers, in part, to providing for them in their old age. How this is lived out varies from family to family. Some parents want to be in touch with their family daily while others prefer more distance and independence.

Doug and I brought his mom home to live with us after she suffered a stroke that left her with dementia. It was the hardest year of my life and we couldn't have done it without the help of extended family. But we believed it was the best choice for her and we were glad we could do it. I have a friend whose parents lived on the opposite coast from her. Honoring her parents meant calling them often and using her vacation to visit them. It's still a long way off, but my son says he'll find the best nursing home for me that he can afford! And that'll be okay if that's where God wants me.

My grandpa was an abusive alcoholic. My mom had little to do with him during my childhood. But she visited him in the hospital in his last days. The common denominator of these examples is an attitude of respect, forgiveness and love. Pray that God will show you what honoring your parents and grandparents looks like for your family.

**Providing an Income**
1) Look at Proverbs 31:16, 18, 24, and 27. In what occupations was this woman involved?

_____

_____

_____

2) Acts 18:1-3 introduces Priscilla and Aquila. What did Priscilla do for a living?

_____

Working outside the home can be an important way to provide for your family and help your husband. Consider this choice carefully and pray for wisdom. Proverbs 23:4 says, "Do not wear yourself out to get rich; do not trust your own cleverness." Ask God to give you wisdom to know if this is the best option for your family and how many hours you should work.

Pray about the pursuits to which God is calling you. When you are ready, go back to your blueprint and label the interior walls with the long-term priorities that God has laid on your heart. Do this in pencil so you can "remodel" as needed.

You may wonder where all your other interests and responsibilities fit. Or maybe you felt like you needed to draw ten walls! (If you did, keep your eraser handy.) The next section will help, because it's time to decorate.

# Home Building for the Wise Woman

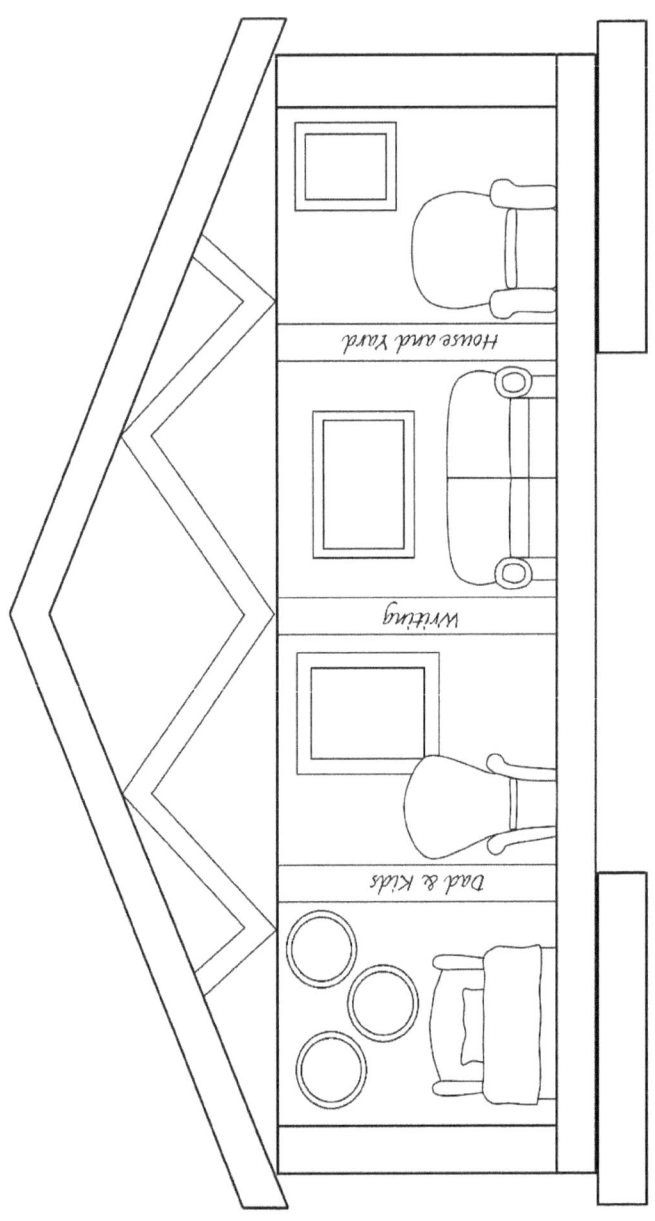

# 6
# Furniture and Décor

*No widow may be put on the list of widows unless she is over sixty, has been faithful to her husband, and is well known for her good deeds, such as bringing up children, showing hospitality, washing the feet of the Lord's people, helping those in trouble and devoting herself to all kinds of good deeds. 1 Timothy 5:9-10*

Doug and I were excited to move into our new house the week before Christmas. It was a crazy time to move, but we couldn't wait any longer! We loved finding art for the walls and furniture for the rooms. They added beauty and comfort to our home.

So far you have planned the framework of your home: the foundation, the bearing walls, the roof, and the interior walls. All of these are God-given priorities, so building them into your life and maintaining them honors him. But what else does God want you to do? Is he leading you to serve at church? Be involved in your community or your children's school? Connect with someone who is lonely? Share a hobby with friends? Does he want you to learn an instrument, paint, or write?

Just as it is unwise to polish the silver while rain is pouring through a hole in the roof, these pursuits should not compromise your relationship with God or your husband. Nor should they hinder your involvement in the activities you wrote on the walls of your blueprint. Nonetheless, these ministries enrich your life, like furniture and decorations beautify your home.

**Serve**

1) Read 1 Timothy 5:9-10 again. Here Paul lists the qualifications of a woman who could be put on the list of widows. For what good deeds was she to be known?

_____

_____

_____

2) In Bible times, washing guests' feet was the job of the servant. What are realistic ways you can serve other believers?

_____

_____

_____

3) Hospitality, at the time of the early Church, involved welcoming the traveler or alienated person into one's home. Do you know someone who has no support system? Someone new to town? What can you do to help?

_____

_____

_____

When I was in second grade, we moved to a rental house in a new neighborhood. Our landlord lived across the road. The day we moved in, he brought us a lemon pie his mother had made. I thought it tasted great, and I didn't even like lemon pie!

4) Are there other good deeds that God has brought to your mind to do? Jot them down to consider.

_____

_____

_____

_____

**Teach**

1) In Titus 2:3-4 older women are instructed to "teach what is good." Whom are they teaching?

_____

2) Look at Proverbs 31:26. For what kind of teaching is this woman known?

_____

_____

As I mentioned earlier, when our kids were babies, I struggled with my attitude toward Doug. At church one Sunday, I approached a woman I thought could give me good advice. I told her how Doug's and my marriage was good, but our parenting was a mess. "Would you like to do a Bible study with me?" she asked. I didn't see what that had to do with my problem, but I said yes. I learned so much from this dear woman over the years! I learned the importance and authority of the Bible, and how to pray about anything and everything. I began the process of developing a gentle and quiet spirit, memorized scripture, and learned how to love my husband and children more. This woman was my mentor, prayer warrior, cheerleader, and friend.

You don't have to be old to be older. And you don't have to be older to be further along in a particular area of life than someone else. Is there someone God has put in your life with whom you can share your knowledge, a skill, or what God has done? This teaching ministry can be a Bible study that spans years or it can be a two-hour coffee break spent talking about how to organize a kitchen.

**Other Interests**
The wife of noble character described in Proverbs 31 had several interests and ministries. See how many you can list. Circle any that resonate with you.

_____

_____

_____

_____

Over the years, my decorating style has changed. Many furniture pieces and decorations have ended up in garage sales. Others are enduring treasures. In life, many opportunities to minister are short-term, or even a one-time deal. Some are long-term, but not permanent. Still others are lifelong pursuits. Pray that God will show you the ministries and interests he wants you to pursue. Write them on the furniture and decorations of your blueprint.

Now that we have planned our foundation, walls, roof, furniture and decorations, what's next? We stop planning and build!

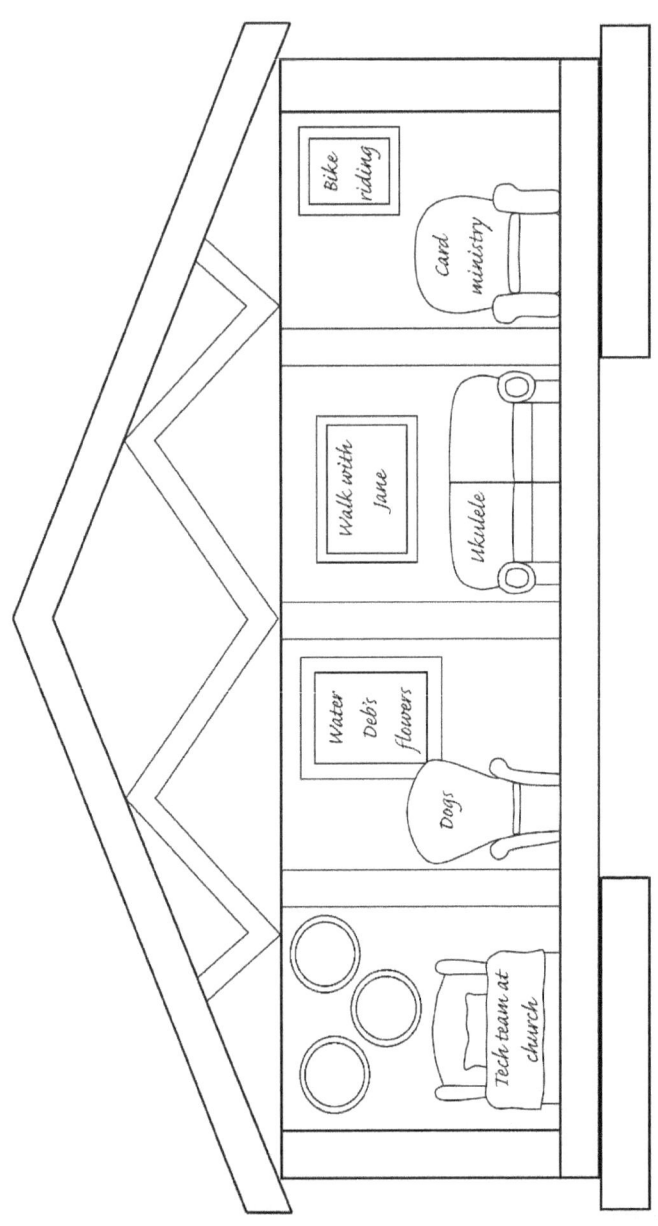

# 7
# Build Your Lovely Home

*By wisdom a house is built, and through understanding it is established; through knowledge its rooms are filled with rare and beautiful treasures. Proverbs 24:3-4*

Throughout this Bible study, you have studied God's priorities for your life. The blueprint you have developed helps you see how they relate to each other. Now, how do you use it to help you wisely build your home?

**Stop Comparing**
One important thing to realize is that you are building *your* home, not anyone else's. Your blueprint is unique, designed just for you and your family. What if the builder Doug and I hired would have said, "This plan isn't like the other houses in this neighborhood. I think you should build it like them."? We'd have said, "No way!" By refusing to compare our lives with others, we go a long way toward eliminating feelings of inadequacy and unfounded guilt.

Look at Galatians 6:4-5. How can we avoid comparing ourselves with others?

_____

_____


The blueprint you have developed is one way for you to test your actions. Use it to remind yourself of your priorities and to decide about opportunities—without worrying about what someone else will think. Romans 14:4 reminds us it is God we should please. He is our master.

## Make Wise Choices

When Doug and I built our house, we drew up the plans ourselves. We planned everything down to where each electrical outlet would go. This planning really helped when it came time to build. Our blueprint provided a clear way to show the builder what we wanted, and it made the process more efficient because all the deciding was done. We could focus on building.

In our culture, we are bombarded with choices. We decide what to eat, what style clothing we wear, what kind of dishes reflect our personality, what movie to watch, what career to follow, what church to join, what brand of car to drive, what color phone to carry. We even have a ridiculous number of dog food brands from which to choose! All these options can make it difficult to manage our time well. It's easy to get distracted from what really matters.

1) Read Proverbs 6:6-8. Who tells the ant what to do?

___

2) When does he store provisions?

___

3) When does he gather food?

___

We can see that the ant in this passage is self-directed, but does he work nonstop? No, he doesn't. But he works at the right time. You can use your blueprint to help you plan the best use of your time.

At the beginning of each week, or day, whichever works for you, think about your blueprint and ask yourself questions about each part of your home. The following are examples to get you started. Your questions will be different based on what you have written on your blueprint.

*Foundation:* Have I had my quiet time with God? How am I doing at listening for God's direction in everything I do? How can I praise and worship him today? What does God want me to do this week?

*Bearing walls:* How am I loving others? Are there areas where I am being self-centered? How can I encourage others? How can I foster love and respect in our home today?

*Roof:* What can I do to help my husband? (Don't forget to ask him.) Have I prayed for him? How can I express my appreciation to him? Am I doing a good job for my boss? Am I respectful of my husband or other authority?

*Interior walls:* What do the kids need today? (Time with me? Encouragement? Help with learning a new skill? Discipline? A note of affirmation?) What do I need to do in the home? How can I improve my performance on the job? Do I have class assignments due?

*Decorations:* What ministries am I committed to this week? Do I need to spend time with my parents? Do the dogs need a bath? When is a good time to work on my painting this week?

## Deal with Sin

When building a house, things don't always go according to plan. The walls are off square or the trim is nicked. Sometimes things are bad enough that the work has to be torn out and redone.

When we evaluate our relationships and ourselves, we are bound to think of areas where we fall short. Don't let that stop you. Embrace the process. God has provided for your shortcomings and sins.

1) Look at 1 John 1:9. What are we told to do when we sin?

_____

_____


2) What is God's response?

_____

_____

_____


The word confess means to admit. We're not asked to work up feelings of sorrow. We are told to admit that what we've done (or thought) is sin. Agree with God about it. The exciting thing is that God doesn't just forgive us, but he also cleanses us. We get a fresh, new start!

## Rely on God

Home building can be daunting at times. It's easy to feel inadequate. Thankfully, we aren't expected to do it on our own.

1) Look at 2 Corinthians 12:9. Paul was tormented by what he called "a thorn in my flesh." Whatever it was, it made his ministry difficult, and he asked God to remove it. What did God say was all Paul needed?

_____

_____

2) How do our weaknesses display God's power?

_____

_____

_____

3) In Philippians 4:13 Paul repeated this idea. What can we do through Jesus' strength?

_____

_____

4) In Deuteronomy 31:6 we find a wonderful promise. How can we face trials with courage?

_____

_____

_____

\*\*\*

If my life were a house, what shape would it be in? Does the roof need repair? Is there so much furniture I can't walk through the house? Are there chips in the walls? Do they need painted? Worse yet, is the foundation crumbling?

Or, is the foundation sturdy, the bearing walls intact, the walls freshly painted, the roof well-maintained? Is the furniture well-placed and in good repair? Is there just the right number of decorations that go well together and make my home beautiful?

When Doug and I moved into our third house, it was bigger than we thought we needed. But we soon discovered that God had a purpose for that extra square footage. We were able to house a missionary family in our basement for seven months, host church-wide events, and accommodate Doug's elderly mother and our adult children.

God knows what he has planned for the home you are building. With the blueprint he and you have designed, you are able to decide about day-to-day activities, and complete the plans God has for your household. Enjoy the building process!

Build Your Lovely Home

## Sample Blueprint

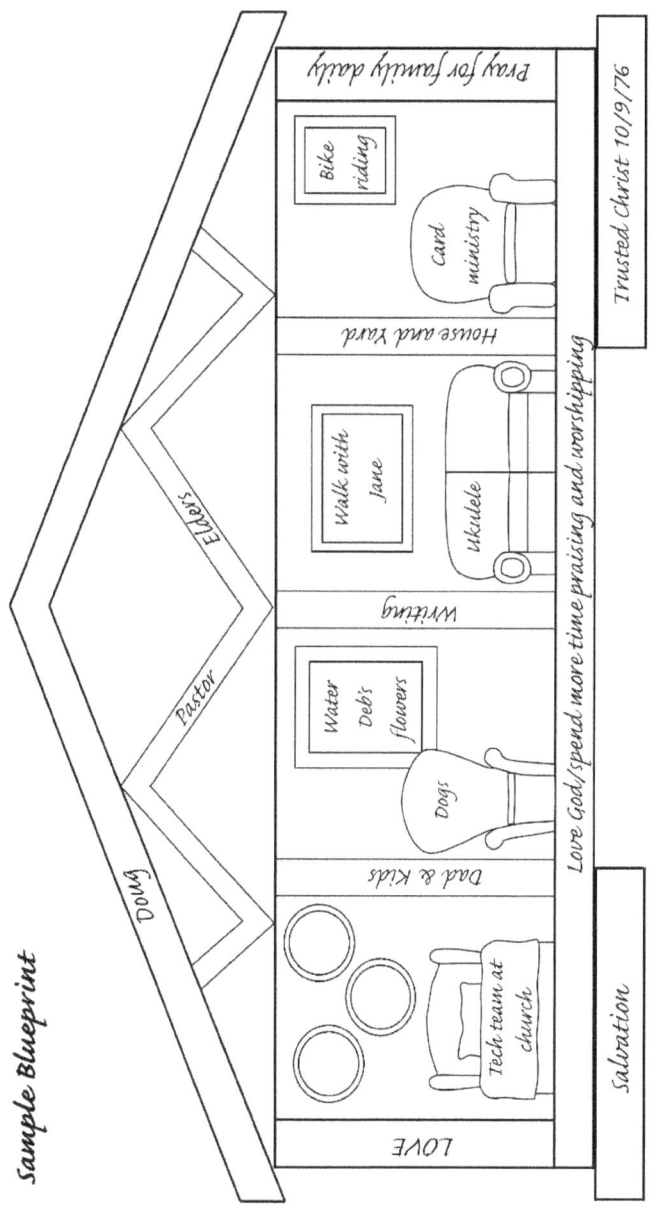

Home Building for the Wise Woman 59

*Your Blueprint*

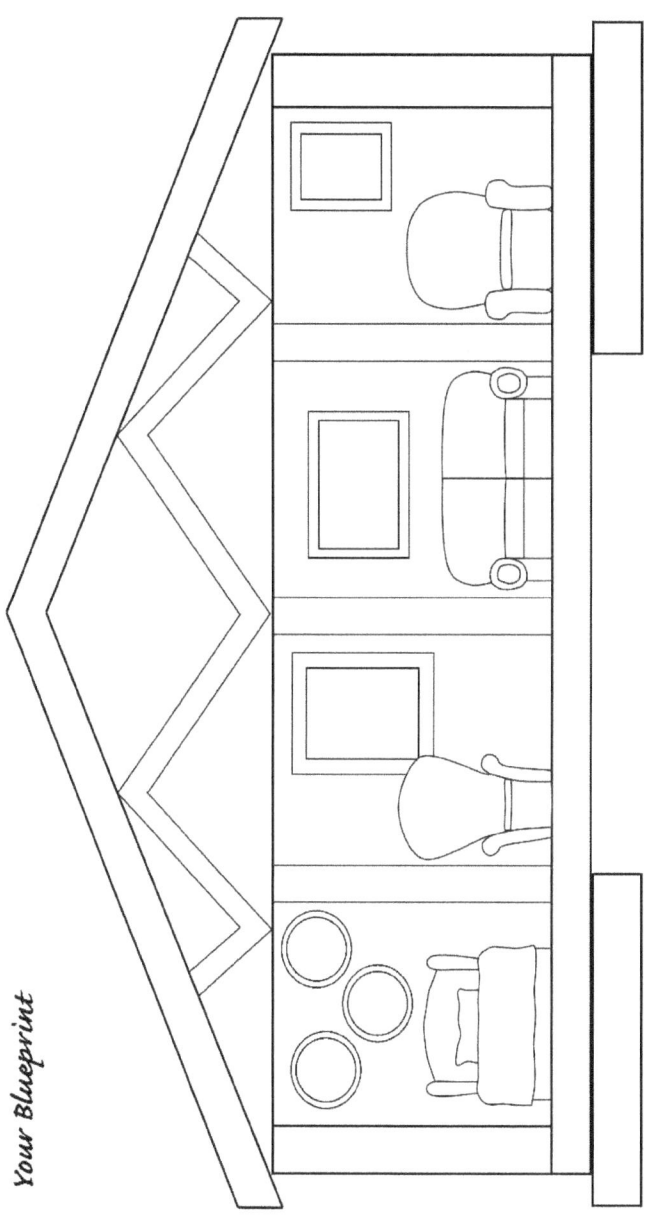

Home Building for the Wise Woman 61

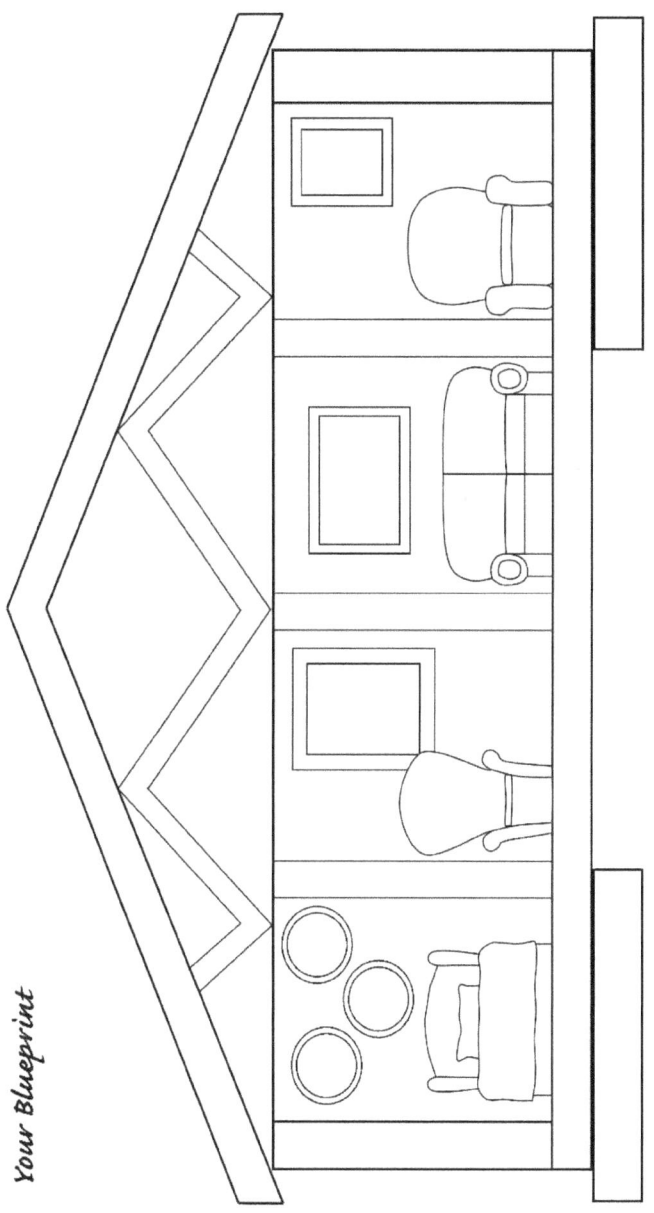

Your Blueprint

www.ingramcontent.com/pod-product-compliance
Lightning Source LLC
Chambersburg PA
CBHW061250040426
42444CB00010B/2333